MOVERS, SHAKERS, & HISTORY MAKERS

R.L. STINE
AUTHOR WITH A FLAIR FOR SCARE

CONTENT CONSULTANT
JAMES BLASINGAME, PhD
PROFESSOR, DEPARTMENT OF ENGLISH
ARIZONA STATE UNIVERSITY

BY MARTHA LONDON

CAPSTONE PRESS
a capstone imprint

Capstone Captivate is published by Capstone Press, an imprint of Capstone.
1710 Roe Crest Drive
North Mankato, Minnesota 56003
www.capstonepub.com

Library of Congress Cataloging-in-Publication Data
Names: London, Martha, author.
Title: R.L. Stine : author with a flair for scare / Martha London.
Description: North Mankato, Minnesota : Capstone Press, [2021] | Series:
  Movers, shakers, and history makers | Includes index. | Audience: Grades
  4-6
Identifiers: LCCN 2020001056 (print) | LCCN 2020001057 (ebook) | ISBN
  9781496684783 (hardcover) | ISBN 9781496688200 (paperback) | ISBN
  9781496684981 (PDF)
Subjects: LCSH: Stine, R. L.—Juvenile literature. | Authors,
  American—20th century—Biography—Juvenile literature. | Children's
  stories—Authorship—Juvenile literature.
Classification: LCC PS3569.T4837 Z76 2021 (print) | LCC PS3569.T4837
  (ebook) | DDC 813/.54—dc23
LC record available at https://lccn.loc.gov/2020001056
LC ebook record available at https://lccn.loc.gov/2020001057

Image Credits
AP Images: Ed Bailey, cover (foreground); Getty Images: Shawn Ehlers/WireImage, 28, Slaven Vlasic/Getty Images Entertainment, 37, Steven A Henry/WireImage, 23; iStockphoto: abalcazar, 15, FairytaleDesign, 34, JR Araujo Photography, 8, spxChrome, 11, undefined undefined, 5; Newscom: Ace Pictures, 31, Luis Santana/Tampa Bay Times/Zuma Press, 42–43, Tom Rodriguez/ZumaPress, 6; Red Line Editorial: 17; Rex Features: Aurora Rose/Starpix/Shutterstock, 38, Ed Bailey/AP/Shutterstock, 24; Shutterstock Images: 88Andrei, 33, f11photo, 7, Featureflash Photo Agency, 39, JHVEPhoto, 21, Popartic, 19, Romolo Tavani, cover (background), 1; Yearbook Library: Seth Poppel, 13

Editorial Credits
Editor: Marie Pearson; Designer: Colleen McLaren; Production Specialist: Ryan Gale

Printed in the United States of America.
PA117

CONTENTS

Words in **bold** are in the glossary.

CHAPTER ONE

GROWING UP SHY

It was the early 1950s, and Bob Stine was 9 years old. Bob's mother kept telling him not to go in the attic. It was just a storage area, she explained, and there was nothing up there that he needed to see. But Bob was curious. He wondered what was up there. He had a big imagination, and the attic made him think of scary monsters. Later, he would use that imagination to write stories.

The idea of monsters in the attic scared Bob, but eventually his curiosity grew too strong. He decided he had to find out what was up there. He opened the attic door. The room was dusty and dark. There was a case in one corner. He opened the lid. Inside the case, Bob found an old typewriter. He realized he could use it to write stories.

As a child, Stine wrote stories on a typewriter he found in his attic. He also spent a lot of time reading.

One of Bob Stine's most popular series is Goosebumps. He has also written books in several other series.

Bob took the typewriter back to his room and began to type. He had so many ideas. The keys clicked and clacked as he wrote them down. His mom told him to go play outside. But Bob had books to write. Sixty-five years later, Bob goes by the name R.L. Stine. He has written more than 330 books for kids. His books are mostly about monsters and solving mysteries.

HUMBLE BEGINNINGS

Robert Lawrence Stine was born October 8, 1943. Today people know him as R.L. Stine. But his friends and family call him Bob. Bob grew up near Columbus, Ohio.

Columbus is in central Ohio. It is Ohio's capital city.

Bob had two younger siblings, a brother and a sister. His mom stayed at home with the kids. Bob's dad worked in a **warehouse**.

When Bob was young, his family did not have a lot of money. His parents worked hard to make sure their kids did not feel poor. But Bob wore clothes that his cousin outgrew. The hand-me-down clothes made Bob feel shy at school. Bob was worried his classmates knew his family was poor.

Listening to the radio was a popular form of entertainment when Stine was growing up. He listened to many stories on the radio.

Although Bob was smart, he struggled in school. He did not like to study or do his homework. Bob did not like physical education class. He did not like playing sports. He preferred to stay indoors. Inside, his imagination ran wild. He loved to read comic books of all kinds, but he especially loved horror stories. Bob's family did not get a TV set until he was 9 years old. Before then, he listened to stories on the radio. Some of the radio shows were funny. Others were scary. Bob could see the whole story in his mind.

BOB'S FAVORITE RADIO SHOWS

- *THE LONE RANGER* (1933–1954) A Western about the adventures of a lawman
- *GANG BUSTERS* (1935–1957) A show that dramatized real FBI cases
- *THE SHADOW* (1937–1954) A show that followed a mysterious person who brought villains to justice
- *THE WHISTLER* (1942–1955) A drama about solving fictional crimes

FINDING HIS PASSION

Bob loved to write. After he found the typewriter, he spent most of his time writing. He wrote everything. He wrote stories and jokes at home. When he got to school, he gave the stories to his classmates.

His teachers took the stories away because they distracted students during class. Even when his teachers took the stories away, Bob kept writing. He made small books with illustrations.

Bob was afraid of a lot of things when he was young. He was especially afraid of the dark. He did not like going down in the dark basement by himself. Bob was also afraid that something might be hiding in the garage. Stories helped him. He could imagine characters beating monsters. He could also write jokes. Laughing helped him feel less afraid.

STORIES ON THE RADIO

One radio show that Bob remembers hearing as a child is *Suspense*. The radio host told scary stories in a dramatic voice. Bob was always too afraid to listen to the whole story. But he would use the host's voice as inspiration for the books he wrote later in his life. He wanted to scare people the way the radio host scared him.

Many children are afraid of the dark and being alone.
So going alone into a dark basement can be scary.

Although Bob was not a very dedicated student, he loved making his classmates laugh. In addition to writing and passing funny notes during class, Bob interrupted class to make jokes. Some of his teachers were not impressed with his behavior.

When Bob was a senior in high school, he wrote a funny skit. His classmates laughed at the jokes in it. Bob knew he had found something he was good at. He wanted to keep writing. He wanted to entertain people.

Stine attended Bexley High School. He wrote for his school's newspaper.

CHAPTER TWO

WRITING AWAY

R.L. Stine graduated from high school in 1961. He knew he wanted to keep writing. Stine went to college. He attended Ohio State University in Columbus, Ohio.

A JOURNALIST

Stine studied **journalism**. He wanted to write for newspapers or magazines. He worked to stay on top of current events. To practice even more, Stine worked at one of Ohio State's student magazines called the *Sundial*. He was an **editor** and writer. The *Sundial* was a humor magazine **published** by students at the school. Stine loved editing the magazine. He had such a good time working on it that he sometimes didn't go to class.

Ohio State University was founded in 1870. Today, it serves more than 60,000 students.

Stine continued to love horror stories. But he did not think he could write that kind of story. He preferred to write humorous stories. Through the *Sundial*, Stine made the students on Ohio State University's **campus** laugh.

Stine knew he was funny. He enjoyed making people laugh. Stine graduated from college in 1965. He wasn't sure what he wanted to do next, but he knew that he wanted to keep writing after college. He also wasn't sure if he should stay in Ohio or move somewhere else.

THE *SUNDIAL*

Stine edited the *Sundial* for three years. The other school publication was called the *Lantern*. It served as the school's newspaper. Stine and the other student writers created a joke version of the *Lantern*. They called it the *Latrine*. Latrine is another word for a toilet.

Stine moved hundreds of miles from Columbus to New York City.

TO NEW YORK CITY

Stine stayed in Ohio for another year. By then he was ready for an adventure, so he packed his bags and headed to New York City in 1967.

Stine decided he wanted to be a full-time writer. There were many opportunities for writers in New York. There were large publishing houses that created books. Many famous magazines were also published in the city. If Stine was going to be a writer, he needed to be in a place where there were opportunities.

Stine had heard stories about New York City. It seemed glamorous. But moving to New York was hard. He thought finding a writing job would be easy, but it wasn't. Stine didn't have a lot of money. He had used most of his savings to get to New York City from Columbus. Stine could not afford much. His apartment was small. He worked hard to find a job. He looked through **ads** in the newspapers. There were few full-time writing jobs available. But Stine said yes to whatever opportunities came his way. He knew he had to work hard to get where he wanted to be.

Time is one of the major magazines based out of New York. The magazine was first published in 1923.

FINDING A JOB

Stine dreamed of writing for well-known magazines. He thought writing for *Time* or the *New Yorker* would be fun. Those magazines captured what life was like for many different people. While he was looking for a full-time job, he worked odd jobs.

FACT

Stine could only afford to eat bologna sandwiches when he first moved to New York.

Stine wrote jokes for bubble gum wrappers. He wrote movie reviews. Some of the jobs were not much fun. But Stine did everything he could to keep writing. It took a while, but Stine finally got a job writing full time for a magazine about soft drinks. It was not the most exciting job, but he kept it because he needed the work and wanted to write for magazines. At the same time, Stine kept his eyes open for other jobs. In December 1968, Stine found an opportunity.

Stine left his job at the soda magazine to work for Scholastic. Scholastic publishes books and magazines for schools and kids. Stine was hired to write for one of its magazines, *Junior Scholastic*. Most of the articles were about history and geography. As Stine worked, his boss could see Stine's talent for making people laugh.

Soon, Stine started a new magazine at Scholastic called *Bananas*. *Bananas* was a humor magazine for middle school students. It was full of jokes kids could tell their friends.

At Scholastic, Stine was able to live his dream of being a magazine writer. Working at Scholastic also opened up other writing opportunities.

Stine enjoyed writing *Bananas*. But he assumed his job at Scholastic would be temporary. Stine was sure he wanted to write for adults. He thought Scholastic would only be a stepping-stone to his next big career move.

CHAPTER THREE

FROM FUNNY TO SCARY

In 1969, Stine got married. His wife, Jane Waldhorn, is also a writer and editor. For several years, Waldhorn was Stine's boss at Scholastic.

In the late 1970s, Stine had been writing for Scholastic for more than 10 years. He had not thought he would be there that long. But he liked his job, and he liked his coworkers. *Bananas* was a success in school libraries.

Then one day, Stine received a call from a children's book editor. She had seen his writing for Scholastic. She asked Stine if he had ever considered writing full-length books for children. Stine said he was not sure. He liked how fast-paced writing for a magazine could be. He was always working on several magazine articles at once, and work was never boring.

Stine and his wife, Jane Waldhorn, posed for a photo in 2015. Waldhorn has worked with Stine on several books.

Stine's first published books were humorous. At first, he did not think he could be a horror writer.

Stine wondered if writing a book would hold his attention in the same way writing for magazines did. But the editor was confident that Stine could think of something. She told him to call her back when he had an idea. Stine started thinking. This was a big opportunity. He had loved writing stories as a kid. It would be fun to finally write a book. Better yet, it was supposed to be a humorous book.

Stine thought of a book. In 1978, *How to Be Funny* was published. Stine wanted the book to be useful to children. *How to Be Funny* was a **nonfiction** guide for kids that gave step-by-step instructions on how to be funny. Stine did not publish the book under his real name. Instead, he used a pen name. He called himself **Jovial** Bob Stine. *Jovial* means "friendly and happy." Jovial Bob Stine would go on to write many more humorous books for kids.

A NEW DIRECTION

In 1985, Stine had a big change in his life. Scholastic had changed some of its goals. As a result, many people lost their jobs. Stine lost his job at Scholastic.

Even though Stine lost his job, he stayed in touch with editors at the company. He had worked there for many years. He had good relationships with his coworkers.

Shortly after losing his job, Stine had lunch with one of the publishers from Scholastic. She asked him if he wanted to write horror novels for teens. That was not something Stine had ever considered. He had just begun to write humorous books for children. And Stine had always considered himself a humorous writer, not a scary one. But just like the previous editor, the publisher was confident Stine could write a scary book for teens.

At lunch, the publisher talked to him about writing a book called *Blind Date*. After lunch was finished, both Stine and the publisher went on their way. The publisher was excited to read Stine's **draft**.

As Stine began to work on *Blind Date*, he thought back to his childhood. He loved reading horror comics. But he had never thought about writing a scary novel for teenagers.

Stine headed to the library. He was sure he could find inspiration there. It had been many years since Stine's trips to the barber shop to read the comics. There had to be more horror novels for teens published since then.

START WITH THE TITLE

Many authors start their books with a character or an idea. They come up with the title last. Stine goes backward. He comes up with a title first. Then he writes a story that matches the title.

Stine discovered he loved writing horror novels. He began writing more scary stories for teenagers.

When Stine got to the library, he was surprised to see there were very few horror books for teens. He brought home the few books he could find. Then he got to work.

Blind Date came out in 1986. In the book, a teenage boy talks to his blind date on the phone. He thinks she seems really interested in him. But things take a nightmarish turn when the two meet in person. It was Stine's first horror novel. He published it under the name R.L. Stine. He enjoyed writing horror. He liked it so much, he decided to stop writing humor.

STINE'S BOOK AWARDS

- CHAMPION OF READING AWARD (2002)
- GUINNESS BOOK OF WORLD RECORDS' BEST-SELLING CHILDREN'S BOOK SERIES AUTHOR (2003)
- THRILLER WRITERS OF AMERICA THRILLERMASTER (2011)
- HORROR WRITERS ASSOCIATION'S BRAM STOKER LIFETIME ACHIEVEMENT AWARD (2013)
- *CHICAGO TRIBUNE* YOUNG ADULT LITERARY AWARD (2016)

Even though Stine enjoyed writing funny stories, he saw that kids liked scary books more. Jovial Bob Stine retired. R.L. Stine started working.

CHAPTER FOUR

WRITING MACHINE

Blind Date was a hit. It became a best seller. Many teens read the book. Teens did not have many options for horror books in the 1980s. They wanted more. Stine continued to write horror novels for teens. In 1989, he started a series called Fear Street. The series is written for teens.

FINDING SUCCESS

In the early 1990s, Stine's wife, Jane Waldhorn, suggested he write scary books for younger readers. The Fear Street series was going strong. But those books were too scary for younger readers. Readers who were 7 to 12 years old had fewer scary book options than teens. Waldhorn believed it was important to provide interesting books for all age levels.

Stine's horror books quickly became a huge success. His Fear Street series was very popular with teenagers.

Stine agreed there was a need. But this was a different audience than he had been writing for. He was worried he would not be able to write a book that was appropriate for younger readers. However, Stine knew he had to try.

In 1992, *Welcome to Dead House* was published. The book is about Amanda and Josh, a sister and brother. They move into a creepy old house in a weird town. They soon realize the house is more than just spooky. It may even be haunted. Amanda and Josh soon find out why it might not be the best idea to make friends in their new town.

ONE-FINGER TYPING

R.L. Stine never learned how to type properly. Even though he began writing stories at a young age, he always used just one finger. Stine is left-handed and has typed all of his books with only his left index finger. He's written so many books this way that his finger is bent now.

Stine's original Goosebumps series has 62 books. He wrote even more Goosebumps books in spin-off series.

Welcome to Dead House was the first book in a new series called Goosebumps. Goosebumps was for children who were not ready for teen books but were too old for books aimed at young kids.

Goosebumps was a success. The books were special not only because they were for younger readers. Goosebumps was targeted at boys and girls equally. In one book, the main character would be a boy. In the next book, a girl was the main character.

Stine includes a lot of supernatural monsters, like werewolves, in his stories for children. Other monsters include mummies and zombies.

Goosebumps was one of the first series to have equal representation for boy characters and girl characters. Stine knew horror stories were for everybody. He wanted to make sure all his readers could see themselves in his books.

There was also a trick to writing scary books for younger audiences. Stine had to make sure kids knew they were always safe. When Stine wrote books for older teens, he had to make it seem like the world in the book was real. But younger audiences need to know that the scary things happening in books are fake. Kids also need to believe they can be their own heroes. So Stine used things such as supernatural monsters that could be beaten by the main characters. Kids always knew the danger in the Goosebumps books couldn't reach them.

The Goosebumps series continued to gain positive attention. The books inspired a TV show called *Goosebumps* that ran for four seasons between 1995 and 1998. Stine was proud of the work he was doing.

A WRITING MACHINE

By the mid-1990s, Stine was writing books for Goosebumps and Fear Street full time. He wrote a book for each series every month. He also began writing novels for adults.

In 1998, Stine began another series of books. He wanted kids to have as many options as possible. Readers were devoted to Stine. They joined monthly book clubs. Readers got a new book each month.

Stine signs a book for a young fan. People of all ages enjoy reading Stine's stories.

Stine (standing, left) and the *Goosebumps* cast make their best frightened expressions at a screening of the film.

Throughout the 1990s and into the 2000s, Stine continued to write books. He never ran out of new ideas. In 2014, Stine's first picture book was published. The book is called *Little Shop of Monsters*. It is a scary story for children 4 to 8 years old.

Meanwhile, the Goosebumps series continued to be successful. *Goosebumps* the movie came out in 2015. The movie's **plot** imagined what would happen if all of the monsters from Stine's books came to life. Two teens and Stine have to save their town from the monsters. Jack Black played Stine in the movie. Black worked with Stine personally. Black wanted to make sure he portrayed Stine respectfully, even if Black chose to change some things about the character.

Jack Black is an actor and comedian who played Stine in the *Goosebumps* film.

After publishing a picture book, Stine wanted more opportunities to work with both words and pictures. It reminded him of his childhood, when he wrote stories with drawings for his classmates. In 2016, Stine began writing story lines for Marvel comic books. In an interview, Stine said it was like going back to where he started. He had first started writing comic books as a kid. It was exciting to be writing for a big company like Marvel. He liked doing something different with the Marvel character, Man-Thing. In other comics, the swamp creature couldn't speak. Stine decided the character should be able to talk in the new comics.

As of 2020, Stine was still writing books for young readers. He writes approximately two to three Goosebumps books each year. More books in the Goosebumps SlappyWorld series were planned to be released in 2020. Stine did not expect his books to be so successful. But kids remember his books even when they grow up. At book events, adults bring copies of the Goosebumps or Fear Street books they read as kids. They ask Stine to sign them.

BEST-SELLING CHILDREN'S BOOK SERIES

This table shows a few of the best-selling children's book series written for an audience similar to the one for Goosebumps. The books are ranked by the number of book copies they had sold by 2018.

- 500 MILLION COPIES: HARRY POTTER BY J.K. ROWLING

- 350 MILLION COPIES: GOOSEBUMPS (INCLUDING SPIN-OFFS) BY R.L. STINE

- 200 MILLION COPIES: DIARY OF A WIMPY KID BY JEFF KINNEY

- MORE THAN 176 MILLION COPIES: THE BABY-SITTERS CLUB BY ANN M. MARTIN

Stine has attended literary events around the country.
He thinks it is important for every child to read.

When he first started meeting his fans who had
grown into adults, Stine was surprised. He did not
think that adults would want to meet the author of
books they read as children.

Today, Stine enjoys meeting his readers. Whether they are 8 years old or 28 years old, Stine likes knowing there are many generations of Goosebumps readers.

TIMELINE

1943: Robert Lawrence Stine is born on October 8.

1965: Stine graduates college.

1975: Stine writes for *Bananas*, a humor magazine for middle school students.

1978: Stine finishes his first full-length book for children, *How to Be Funny*.

1986: Stine writes *Blind Date*, his first teen horror novel.

1989: Stine begins writing the Fear Street series.

1992: Stine's first Goosebumps book, *Welcome to Dead House*, is published.

2014: Stine publishes his first picture book, *The Little Shop of Monsters*.

2016: Stine begins writing for Marvel comics.

2020: Stine continues to write new books for the Goosebumps series.

GLOSSARY

ads (ADS)
advertisements that feature products available to buy or that alert people to job openings

campus (KAM-puhs)
the area where a college's buildings sit

draft (DRAFT)
a new piece of writing that isn't the final version

editor (EH-duh-ter)
someone who helps an author shape a book into its final form

journalism (JER-nu-li-sum)
the act of writing news articles for sources such as newspapers and magazines

nonfiction (non-FIK-shuhn)
written works about real people, places, objects, or events

plot (PLOT)
the main story in a piece of writing or a movie

published (PUH-blishd)
a book released to the public by a company or organization

warehouse (WARE-hows)
a large building where people store materials

READ MORE

Payne, M.D. *Who Is R.L. Stine?* New York: Penguin Workshop, 2019.

Purslow, Neil. *The Spooky World of R.L. Stine.* New York: Smartbook Media, 2017.

Stabler, David. *Kid Authors: True Tales of Childhood from Famous Writers.* Philadelphia: Quirk Books, 2017.

INTERNET SITES

About R.L. Stine
http://rlstine.com/about-rl-stine

How Do You Publish a Book?
https://www.wonderopolis.org/wonder/how-do-you
-publish-a-book

A Video Interview with R.L. Stine
https://www.readingrockets.org/books/interviews/stine

INDEX